THE CARIBBEAN
TODAY

TRINIDAD & TOBAGO

Tobago

Little Tobago

Buccoo Reef

Scarborough

Caribbean Sea

11°00'

11°0

Galera Point

VENEZUELA

Dragons Mouths

NORTHERN RANGE

★ Port-of-Spain • Tunapuna

Arima

Matura Bay

Caroni

10°30'

10°3

• Chaguanas

Gulf of Paria

Trinidad

Cocos Bay

Guataro Point

CENTRAL RANGE

San Fernando •

Ortoire

ATLANTIC OCEAN

Point Fortin •

Galeota Point

10°00'

10°0

Serpents Mouth

VENEZUELA

0   25 Miles

0   25 Kilometers

THE CARIBBEAN
TODAY

TRINIDAD & TOBAGO

Romel Hernandez

Mason Crest Publishers
Philadelphia

Produced by OTTN Publishing, Stockton, N.J.

Mason Crest Publishers
370 Reed Road
Broomall, PA 19008
www.masoncrest.com

3 5 7 9 8 6 4 2
Library of Congress Cataloging-in-Publication Data

Hernandez, Romel.
   Trinidad and Tobago / Romel Hernandez.
      p. cm. — (The Caribbean today)
   Includes index.
   ISBN 978-1-4222-0629-4 (hardcover) — ISBN 978-1-4222-0696-6 (pbk.)
   1. Trinidad and Tobago—Juvenile literature. [1. Trinidad and Tobago.] I. Title.
   F2119.H47 2008
   972.983—dc22
                                                2008032735

THE CARIBBEAN
TODAY

Bahamas
Barbados
Cuba
Dominican Republic
Haiti

Caribbean Islands:
Facts & Figures

Jamaica
Leeward Islands
Puerto Rico
Trinidad & Tobago
Windward Islands

Table of Contents

Discovering the Caribbean

James D. Henderson

THE CARIBBEAN REGION is a lovely, ethnically diverse part of tropical America. It is at once a sea, rivaling the Mediterranean in size; and it is islands, dozens of them, stretching along the sea's northern and eastern edges. Waters of the Caribbean Sea bathe the eastern shores of Central America's seven nations, as well as those of the South American countries Colombia, Venezuela, and Guyana. The Caribbean islands rise, like a string of pearls, from its warm azure waters. Their sandy beaches, swaying palm trees, and balmy weather give them the aspect of tropical paradises, intoxicating places where time seems to stop.

But it is the people of the Caribbean region who make it a unique place. In their ethnic diversity they reflect their homeland's character as a crossroads of the world for more than five centuries. Africa's imprint is most visible in peoples of the Caribbean, but so too is that of Europe. South and East Asian strains enrich the Caribbean ethnic mosaic as well. Some islanders reveal traces of the region's first inhabitants, the Carib and Taino Indians, who flourished there when Columbus appeared among them in 1492.

Though its sparkling waters and inviting beaches beckon tourists from around the globe, the Caribbean islands provide a significant portion of the world's sugar, bananas, coffee, cacao, and natural fibers. They are strategically important also, for they guard the Panama Canal's eastern approaches.

The Caribbean possesses a cultural diversity rivaling the ethnic kaleidoscope that is its human population. Though its dominant culture is Latin American, defined by languages and customs bequeathed it by Spain and France, significant parts of the Caribbean bear the cultural imprint of

Palm trees line one of the beautiful beaches of Trinidad.

Northwestern Europe: Denmark, the Netherlands, and most significantly, Britain.

So welcome to the Caribbean! These lavishly illustrated books survey the human and physical geography of the Caribbean, along with its economic and historical development. Geared to the needs of students and teachers, each of the eleven volumes in the series contains a glossary of terms, a chronology, and ideas for class reports. And each volume contains a recipe section featuring tasty, easy-to-prepare dishes popular in the countries dealt with. Each volume is indexed, and contains a bibliography featuring web sources for further information.

Whether old or young, readers of the eleven-volume series DISCOVERING THE CARIBBEAN will come away with a new appreciation of this tropical sea, its jewel-like islands, and its fascinating and friendly people!

Trinidad and Tobago are the southernmost islands of the Caribbean archipelago; geologically, they are considered part of South America. (Opposite) Several buildings nestle among lush mountains on the island of Tobago. The island is part of a chain of volcanic mountains. (Right) Tourists enjoy the beaches of Tobago.

1 A Diverse Pair of Islands

TWO QUITE DIFFERENT islands make up the country of Trinidad and Tobago. The islands were even created differently. Trinidad separated from the mainland of South America 10,000 or more years ago, while the smaller Tobago was once part of an underwater volcanic mountain range connected to the continent.

Trinidad and Tobago form the tail end of the island chain known as the Lesser Antilles, at the southern extreme of the West Indies. The country's climate is tropical—hot and humid, and rainy during the wet season, which lasts from June to December. The northeast *trade winds* cool the islands, however, and the average year-round temperature is around 80° Fahrenheit (27° Celsius). While hurricanes do occasionally strike, the islands lie south of the usual storm path. In 1963, Hurricane Flora slammed the islands, devastating the smaller island of Tobago.

Trinidad is 16 times larger than Tobago, which often feels overshadowed by its big neighbor. But each island offers distinctive natural features.

The Island of Trinidad

Trinidad is situated only 7 miles (11 kilometers) off the coast of Venezuela. More than 10,000 years ago, a land bridge connected the island with the mainland of South America. Today, the island is separated from the continent by the Gulf of Paria.

Two heavily forested mountain ranges stretch across the northern and southern parts of the island. El Cerro del Aripo, located in the larger Northern Range, is the highest peak on the island at 3,084 feet (940 meters). The island's central interior consists of a third mountain range along with rolling plains and swamps filled with coconut and mangrove trees.

The country's capital and main *metropolitan area*, Port of Spain, is located at the northwest end of the island. San Fernando, the biggest city in the south, is the hub of the island's booming oil industry. The island's economy is heavily dependent on oil, which is plentiful in the south as well as in surrounding waters.

Trinidad's most popular tourist beaches are located on the north coast. Leatherback turtles make their nests along the more secluded beaches.

Off the northwest coast of the island are the Bocas—tiny *islets* that got their name from the explorer Christopher Columbus, who dubbed the treacherous waters surrounding them the *Bocas del Dragón* ("mouths of the dragon").

The Nariva Swamp on the eastern coast is home to many exotic animal species, including caimans (a cousin to the crocodile), macaws, and red howler monkeys, whose piercing yelps can be heard miles away.

Trinidad is dotted with mud volcanoes, small mounds that spew sulfuric mud (and that technically aren't volcanoes). Mud-volcano eruptions usually rise only a few feet, but occasionally a particularly violent eruption will occur. In 1997, a mud volcano near the south-central town of Piparo blew, sending mud hundreds of feet into the air and burying many homes.

An unusual feature of Trinidad's landscape is Pitch Lake, near the southwest coast. At 114 acres (46 hectares), this lake of natural *asphalt* is the largest of only three like it in the entire world. Some call it the ugliest tourist attraction in the

A mud volcano at Devil's Woodyard, Trinidad.

Quick Facts: The Geography of Trinidad and Tobago

Location: between the Caribbean Sea and the North Atlantic Ocean, northeast of Venezuela

Area: (slightly smaller than Delaware)
  total: 1,980 square miles (5,128 sq km)
  land: 1,980 square miles (5,128 sq km)
  water: 0 square miles

Borders: none

Climate: tropical with a rainy season from June to December

Terrain: plains with some hills and low mountains

Elevation extremes:
  lowest point: Caribbean Sea—0 feet
  highest point: El Cerro del Aripo—3,084 feet (940 meters)

Natural hazards: infrequent hurricanes and tropical storms

Source: Adapted from CIA World Factbook 2001.

country, but visitors still travel there to take a stroll on the lake's squishy, tar-like surface.

Natural Features of Tobago

Tobago is a small island located 20 miles (32 km) northeast of Trinidad. It is just 26 miles (42 km) across and 9 miles (14 km) wide. For the most part, early European explorers and settlers ignored Tobago. Columbus sighted the island from his ship but decided not to stop.

Although there is some dispute, certain scholars believe Tobago inspired the island setting of *Robinson Crusoe*, a famous 18th-century English novel about a shipwrecked sailor. Lush forests cover the island's rolling hills.

Some of the world's most stunning coral reefs surround Tobago. In these waters, snorkelers get an opportunity to swim through crystal blue waters alongside sleek manta rays.

While Tobago promotes tourism more heavily than does Trinidad, the island as a whole is far less developed than its larger neighbor. Tobago's largest town, Scarborough, is located on the southern coast.

Countless hummingbirds zip through the air of the Tobago Forest Reserve on the northern coast. This hilly rain forest was declared a *reserve* by the British in 1776, making it the oldest environmentally protected forest in the Americas.

Sheet coral in Speyside Bay, off the coast of Tobago. The coral lines the area where a reef slopes off into deeper water.

(Opposite) A cove in Trinidad, where Native Americans may have lived as early as 3,000 years ago. (Right) Fort King George, built at Scarborough, Tobago, in the 1770s, overlooks the ocean. Great Britain claimed Trinidad in the early 17th century; the country remained part of the British Empire until 1962.

2 A Unique and Fascinating History

CHRISTOPHER COLUMBUS CLAIMED the islands of Trinidad and Tobago for Spain in 1498. Some 464 years later, after a long and often painful history as colonies of various European powers, Trinidad and Tobago tasted freedom once again. What happened in between—plus the many changes the country has experienced since gaining its independence—constitutes a unique and fascinating story.

The Arawaks and Caribs

The earliest inhabitants of Trinidad and Tobago probably sailed over from the South American continent around 3,000 years ago. The Arawak tribe had established a sophisticated civilization on Trinidad by about 300 B.C. They called the island Iere, or "land of the hummingbird." These peaceful people lived in highly structured villages headed by chieftains called *caciques*. They hunted, fished, and farmed for food. The staple of their diet was a root called *cassava*, which they used to make bread.

Around A.D. 1400 another South American tribe called the Caribs began migrating from the continent. The Caribs were fierce warriors who used poison arrows to battle the Arawaks. Today, these two tribes, and America's Indian peoples generally, are grouped together under one term: *Amerindians*.

Christopher Columbus was on his third visit to what became known to Europeans as the New World when he arrived at Trinidad on July 31, 1498. At the time, as many as 30,000 Arawaks and Caribs lived on the island.

After sighting three mountain peaks on its southern end, Columbus named the island Trinidad for the Christian Holy Trinity: God the Father, the Son (Jesus), and the Holy Spirit. These peaks are still called the Trinity Hills. Columbus christened Trinidad's smaller neighbor Bellaforma, or "beautiful form," but he didn't land on the island today known as Tobago.

Columbus's journal recounts the beauty the Spanish explorers saw as they sailed along Trinidad's coast. "In all the coast we found that groves of trees went right down to the sea—the fairest thing that eyes have seen," Columbus wrote.

The Legend of El Dorado

Spain named a governor to Trinidad in 1530, but attempts to establish permanent settlements failed. Around this time, European explorers began to spread fantastic stories about the existence of El Dorado, a city made of gold that was said to be somewhere in South America.

The promise of vast riches rekindled the interest of Spanish *conquistadors* in Trinidad. Because of its strategic position just off the continent's coast, the conquistadors saw the island as an ideal launching pad for expeditions searching for El Dorado.

In 1592 Domingo de Vera founded St. Joseph, the island's first capital. Three years later the English explorer Sir Walter Raleigh landed in Trinidad and burned down St. Joseph on his way to search for El Dorado.

No one found the fabled city. But the possibility of its existence promoted Trinidad's early development.

The clash between Spain and England over Trinidad established a pattern that would continue for 200 years. Trinidad and Tobago became a flash point as the European powers of Spain, England, France, and Holland vied for control.

In 1595 the English adventurer Sir Walter Raleigh landed at Trinidad while exploring South America in search of the fabled city of El Dorado. While there Raleigh's men attacked the Spanish settlement at St. Joseph, burning it to the ground.

A Tale of Two Islands

Spain maintained its hold on Trinidad following Raleigh's destruction of St. Joseph. But the country did little to develop the island at first.

The Spaniards forced the island's Amerindians to work on their farms, most of which grew cocoa. These workers revolted against Spanish rule in 1699, killing mission priests and the governor in what became known as the Arena Massacre. The Spaniards swiftly tracked down and executed the rebels.

By the 1700s French farmers had moved to the island with Spain's blessing. They took over many plantations. To replace the dwindling number of Amerindian workers, who were killed off by fighting and disease, slaves were imported from Africa.

In 1797 British warships seized control of Trinidad from Spain. The British would hold on to the island, which soon developed into a solid sugar producer for the empire, until independence came in the 20th century.

Tobago merited less interest from Europeans than did Trinidad. Nevertheless, the island changed hands between colonial powers numerous times.

In 1608 King James I claimed the island for England. Over the next 50 years, British, Dutch, and Courlanders (people who came from the Baltic Sea region in what is today Latvia) fought among themselves to gain the upper hand on Tobago. The French laid claim to the island in 1667 and joined in the fighting. The various countries competing for control raided one another's settlements repeatedly over the years. To add to the trouble and confusion,

Tobago also became a favorite hiding spot for the ruthless pirates who roamed the West Indies.

In 1704 Tobago was declared a neutral no-man's-land—the possession of no country—but the fighting continued. During the American Revolutionary War, the American colonies even tried to seize the island from Great Britain.

In 1815 the fight over Tobago finally ended when France abandoned its claims on the island and formally acknowledged English control in the Treaty of Paris. Tobago, like Trinidad 18 years earlier, became a British colony.

Unity and Independence

Great Britain abolished slavery in its colonies, including Trinidad and Tobago, in 1834. The move was celebrated across the world (although the United States maintained slavery for another 30 years), but it struck a harsh blow to the islands' economies by creating a labor shortage on the plantations.

Plantation owners in Trinidad and Tobago began to import thousands of *indentured* laborers from India. In exchange for passage across the seas, indentured laborers signed restrictive contracts that bound them to work for someone for a specified period of time (typically five years). At the end of that time, they would receive a small piece of land or passage back to their home country. Although the indentured laborers who came from India to work on plantations in Trinidad and Tobago lived in harsh conditions, many eventually settled on the islands rather than return home. The massive immigration of workers to the islands didn't cease until 1917, by which time about 144,000 East Indians, as they are known, had moved to Trinidad and Tobago.

In 1888 Britain decided it would be simpler to govern Trinidad and Tobago as one, so it joined the two neighboring islands politically for the first time. Over most of the next century the leaders of the islands remained predominantly white, despite the fact that the vast majority of the country's population was black and Indian. In addition, critical decisions about the country were made an ocean away in London.

During the 20th century a movement for independence gained momentum. In the 1950s, a formidable leader and spokesman for independence emerged. His name was Eric Williams.

Williams (1911–1981) had been born into a middle-class black Trinidadian family and earned a scholarship to attend Oxford University in England. He became a professor at Howard University in Washington, D.C., and wrote many books, including a history of Trinidad and Tobago.

Eric Williams speaks in London, circa 1961. Williams was instrumental in achieving Trinidad and Tobago's freedom from British rule; he served as the country's prime minister for 20 years.

But Williams wanted to make a difference in his native country, so he returned home. He declared in a famous speech: "I was born here, and here I stay, with the people of Trinidad and Tobago, who educated me free of charge for nine years at Queen's Royal College and for five years at Oxford, who have made me whatever I am, and who have been or might be at any time the victims of the very pressure which I have been fighting against. . . . I am going to let down my bucket where I am, right here with you in the British West Indies."

Williams founded the People's National Movement, a new political party that pushed for independence. In 1962, when Trinidad and Tobago finally gained its independence, Williams became prime minister. He held that position for 20 years.

In the 1970s international oil prices skyrocketed. Because Trinidad had developed into a major oil producer, the country suddenly became flooded with money. Williams expanded the size of government programs and launched ambitious projects to improve the standard of living. But he also came under criticism for spending recklessly or failing to address the needs of the poor.

Williams died in 1981 while he was still serving as prime minister. Many in Trinidad and Tobago today regard him as the father of their nation.

Today's Trinidad and Tobago

After the death of Eric Williams, Trinidad and Tobago struggled. The country's prosperity was closely linked to oil, and a drop in worldwide oil prices devastated the economy. Unemployment on Trinidad and Tobago soared. Crime jumped as drug trafficking increased.

In 1990 a group of Muslim extremists staged a *coup*, seeking to overthrow the democratically elected government. The group, calling itself Jamaat al Muslimeen, stormed the main government buildings in Port of Spain and took hostages, including Prime Minister Arthur N. R. Robinson. By the time government soldiers put down the revolt a few days later, 30 people had been

Basdeo Panday (right) meets with Jacques Chirac, president of France, 2000. The first person of East Indian descent to serve as Trinidad and Tobago's prime minister, Panday held office from 1995 until 2001.

killed and widespread rioting and looting had caused extensive damage to the capital.

The 1990s saw great economic reforms and improvements. The government reduced its involvement in the economy by cutting regulations and encouraging more private investment. The country also diversified its economy to reduce its reliance on oil production. At the same time, oil prices went back up, bringing more money into Trinidad and Tobago's economy.

In 1995 the country marked a historic milestone when Basdeo Panday became the first citizen of East Indian descent to be elected prime minister. While Panday's election was a breakthrough for the nation, blacks and Indians have remained divided politically since the country became independent. Today, most Indians back the United National Congress, while blacks support the People's National Movement, which their hero Williams started.

Panday remained in office until 2001, when a national election resulted in a tie between the two major parties. Eventually, Patrick Manning of the People's National Movement was declared prime minister. Panday bitterly contested the results and called for a new election. The political conflict divided the country along racial lines and threatened the newfound prosperity and stability Trinidad and Tobago had enjoyed for much of the previous decade.

The People's National Movement was re-elected in 2007, but did not capture the majority of parliament seats that Manning needed to pass his planned constitutional reform.

(Opposite) Merchants sell fresh produce at a stand in Scarborough, Tobago. (Right) A buffalo-drawn cart carries sugarcane, Trinidad. Agriculture remains a small but important part of Trinidad and Tobago's economy.

3 Boom and Bust in an Oil-Based Economy

THE CARIBBEAN'S EARLY European explorers came in search of gold and riches. Discovering no gold—and little else of interest—in Trinidad and Tobago, they mostly ignored the islands for 100 years after Columbus.

Unknown to them, vast riches lay beneath their feet. Of course, it wouldn't be until several centuries later, with the development of industrial economies, that oil would become such a valuable commodity.

Colonial Plantations

By the early 1700s the Europeans who colonized the islands in search of gold had discovered the potential of the rich and fertile soil. Following years of neglect, they established sprawling plantations devoted to the cultivation of tobacco, cocoa, and sugarcane.

At first, the native Arawak and Carib Indians provided the main source of labor, but fighting and sickness dramatically reduced their numbers. In the 1700s, French plantation owners imported thousands of African slaves to work on their estates. After slavery was abolished on the islands in 1834, thousands of indentured laborers were brought over from India to work the fields.

Economic Overview

Today, agriculture remains a small but significant part of Trinidad and Tobago's economy. Trinidad's central and eastern plains produce sugarcane and coconuts. Other major agricultural products include cocoa, rice, citrus fruits, coffee, vegetables, and poultry.

An estimated 4 percent of Trinidad and Tobago's workforce is involved in farming, but agriculture accounts for less than 1 percent of the country's *gross domestic product (GDP)*. GDP—the total value of goods and services produced annually—is an important measure of the overall size of a nation's economy. Trinidad and Tobago's economy is relatively small. IIn 2007 the World Bank, an international development-assistance organization, estimated Trinidad and Tobago's GDP at $20.31 billion, which placed the country 112th among the world's nations, on par with the eastern European country of Albania. By comparison, Venezuela—Trinidad and Tobago's nearest neighbor on the South American continent—had an estimated 2007 GDP of almost $334 billion.

However, because GDP is closely linked to population (more people generate more economic activity), it is of limited use in gauging the relative prosperity of a nation's citizens. A more accurate picture is provided by GDP per capita. This statistic, computed by dividing GDP by total population, represents each citizen's average share of a nation's economic activity.

In 2007 GDP per capita in Trinidad and Tobago stood at an estimated $14,100—58th among the world's nations. By the standards of the United States and other Western industrialized countries, $14,100 is not a lot of money. For example, GDP per capita in Great Britain—Trinidad and Tobago's

An offshore oil platform with 17 pumps off Galeota Point, Trinidad. Oil and oil-related products make up nearly half of Trinidad and Tobago's annual exports.

former colonial master—was about $43,000 in 2007. But worldwide, Trinidad and Tobago ranks as a middle-income nation. It is, in fact, more prosperous than Venezuela, whose estimated GDP per capita in 2007 stood at $7,320.

Nevertheless, Trinidad and Tobago's economy has certain persistent problems. Unemployment remains an issue, estimated at 6.5 percent in 2007. In addition, a fairly large percentage of the population lives below the government-established poverty line—nearly one in five, according to the latest available statistics.

Tourism

Both islands support a healthy tourist trade, with about 3 percent of the country's gross domestic product coming from the tourism industry. Trinidad's Carnival draws thousands of partygoers from around the world who come to revel in the renowned festival's music and wild costumes. Tobago's pristine beaches and forests attract many eco-tourists interested in exploring the island's stunning natural environment and wildlife.

Tourists watch a small fishing boat, Trinidad.

Quick Facts: The Economy of Trinidad and Tobago

Gross domestic product (GDP*):
$20.31 billion (2007)
GDP per capita: $14,100
Inflation: 7.9%
Natural resources: petroleum, natural gas, asphalt
Agriculture (0.6% of GDP): cocoa, rice, citrus, coffee, vegetables; poultry (2007 est.)
Services (37.5% of GDP): tourism (2000 est.)
Industry (61.9% of GDP): petroleum, chemicals, tourism, food processing, cement, beverages, cotton textiles

Foreign trade:
Exports—$12.02 billion: petroleum and petroleum products, liquefied natural gas, methanol, ammonia, urea, steel products, beverages, cereal, sugar, cocoa, coffee, citrus fruit, vegetables, flowers
Imports—$7.485 billion: mineral fuels, lubricants, machinery, transportation equipment, manufactured goods, food, live animals, grain
Currency exchange rate: 6.22 Trinidad and Tobago dollars (TTD) = U.S. $1 (July 2008)

*GDP = total value of goods and services produced in a year. Figures are 2007 estimates unless otherwise indicated. Sources: CIA World Factbook 2008; World Bank; Bloomberg.com.

Oil Boom

Trinidad and Tobago hasn't needed to promote tourism as heavily as other West Indies countries because of its most valuable natural resource: oil. Trinidad's first oil well was drilled in 1857, but it would be nearly 50 years before the country looked to exploit the "black gold" hidden beneath its ground.

The global demand for oil increased dramatically after the automobile was invented in the early 1900s. By the 1930s, oil was Trinidad and Tobago's main export. In the 1950s, oil companies began drilling for oil in the waters off Trinidad's coast; today most of the country's oil comes from these offshore sites.

The country's oil fields and refineries are located in the southern part of Trinidad. The city of San Fernando serves as the industry's business headquarters.

In the 1970s Trinidad and Tobago enjoyed a period of unprecedented prosperity. A global energy crisis quadrupled oil prices, and the country suddenly got rich. With its profits from oil, the country undertook massive public works projects, spending millions to build highways, housing, and government buildings. "Money," Prime Minister Eric Williams famously remarked, "is no problem."

The boom times didn't last, however. In the late 1980s oil prices bottomed out. Trinidad and Tobago's economy, dependent as it was on the oil industry, went into a tailspin. The unemployment rate more than doubled, to nearly 20 percent.

Comeback

In recent years the government has taken steps to diversify and grow the economy. These steps included *privatizing* state-run businesses and attracting more foreign investment. The government also encouraged the development of new types of businesses to reduce Trinidad and Tobago's dependence on oil and gas production.

Today, although oil and oil-related products still represent about half of the country's exports, Trinidad and Tobago has stepped up production of methanol, natural gas, and asphalt. About 58 percent of the country's exports head to the United States. Other major markets for Trinidad and Tobago's exports include Jamaica, the nations of Latin America, the European Union, and the Caribbean Community (CARICOM), an organization whose goals include the promotion of economic integration among its 14 member-states.

Thanks to economic reforms, *inflation* in Trinidad and Tobago has been under control, and unemployment, though still relatively high, fell to about 6.5 percent in 2007. Residents hope for continued improvement in the nation's economy.

A tourist guide at the Asa Wright Nature Centre, near Arima, Trinidad, makes bird calls while relaxing in a natural pool. (Right) A woman wears an elaborate gold costume in a Carnival competition in Port of Spain. Carnival is one of the most popular celebrations on Trinidad.

4 A Patchwork Quilt: The Culture and People

THE PEOPLE OF Trinidad and Tobago refer to themselves as Trinibagonians. But the nation is far more diverse than the difference between two islands.

Trinidad and Tobago's culture is like a colorful quilt, with pieces drawn from the native Arawak and Carib tribes; Spanish, French, and British colonial influences; and the African slaves and Indian immigrants brought over to work the plantations. This multiculturalism helps make the country special, but it also has been a source of conflict over the years.

Tribes and Explorers

Before Christopher Columbus landed on Trinidad in 1498, the islands were home to rival Amerindian tribes—the Arawaks and the Caribs. The

Arawaks lived peacefully for centuries, but about 100 years before Columbus arrived, the warlike Caribs invaded and established their own villages.

These two tribes fought among themselves, but they met a common foe when the Spanish conquistadors arrived and swiftly overwhelmed them with superior firepower and deadly diseases to which the Amerindians had no immunity. Despite being virtually wiped out by the twin scourges of war and disease, the *indigenous* people of Trinidad and Tobago remain a point of pride for the country.

Native traditions have largely faded, but many on the island strive to keep these traditions alive. During the annual Santa Rosa Festival in Arima, local Carib leaders hold a ritual smoke ceremony to offer thanks and to bless the community. The festival draws people from across the country and reminds them of the Amerindians who called the islands home centuries before Columbus arrived.

Many countries fought for control of Trinidad and Tobago throughout the country's early history. The islands changed hands numerous times among the Spanish, British, French, and Dutch. The islands were exposed to many European cultures, establishing traditions that continue to thrive today.

For example, Trinidad incorporated Carnival traditions from the French. The Christmas tradition of roving bands of musicians playing *parang* comes from Spain. When the islands gained independence in 1962, the country adopted a parliamentary form of government based on the British system.

The official language today is English, but the unofficial language of the country is Trini. This way of speaking is a blend called a *patois*—mostly

Quick Facts: The People of Trinidad and Tobago

Population: 1,047,366

Ethnic groups: Indian (South Asian) 40%, African 37.5%, mixed 20.5%, other 1.2%, unspecified 0.8%

Age structure:
0–14 years: 19%
15–64 years: 71.8%
65 years and over: 9.2%

Population growth rate: 0.891%

Birth rate: 13.22 births/1,000 population

Death rate: 10.93 deaths/1,000 population

Infant mortality rate: 23.59 deaths/1,000 live births

Life expectancy at birth:
total population: 67 years
male: 66.07 years
female: 67.98 years

Total fertility rate: 1.73 children born per woman

Religions: Roman Catholic, 26%; Hindu, 22.5%; Anglican 7.8%, Baptist 7.2%, Pentecostal 6.8%, Muslim 5.8%, Seventh Day Adventist 4%, other Christian 5.8%, other 10.8%, unspecified 1.4%, none 1.9% (2000 est.)

Languages: English (official), Caribbean Hindustani (dialect of Hindi), French, Spanish, Chinese.

Literacy rate (age 15 and over who can read and write): 98.6% (2003 est.)

All figures are 2008 estimates unless otherwise indicated. Source: CIA World Factbook 2008.

English, with Hindi, African, and French words and expressions mixed in. Trini is heavily accented and different enough from Standard English that a tourist visiting the islands for the first time would struggle to follow a conversation between two natives.

African Traditions

When the indigenous population became too small to support Trinidad and Tobago's rapidly expanding plantations, Europeans imported thousands of slaves from Africa to work on their estates. It wasn't long before Africans

A bride and groom at a Hindu wedding, Tunapuna, Trinidad. Hindus make up almost one-quarter of the population of Trinidad and Tobago.

far outnumbered any other racial group on the islands. Today, 40 percent of Trinidad and Tobago's population is black.

These slaves brought their own languages and traditions. They retained their African culture, incorporating it into island culture. Carnival—a celebration associated with Christianity yet accompanied by African-influenced music, dance, and costumes—is a prime example of this rich combination. Carnival takes place on the two days before Ash Wednesday, the start of the Christian season of Lent, a solemn time of fasting and prayer.

The holiday was brought to the country by French Catholics in the 1700s, but African slaves molded it into today's free-for-all party. During Carnival the streets of Port of Spain fill up with drumming and dancing. The revelers paint their bodies wild colors and dress in flamboyant costumes and masks. Other cities—especially Rio de Janeiro and

New Orleans—throw huge Carnival celebrations, but Trinidad boasts that it has the best party of them all.

A unique aspect of Trinidad's Carnival is the assortment of characters that roam the streets. These include, among many others, Jab Jab, the pitchfork-wielding devil; Moko Jumbie, the stilt walker; and Dame Lorraine the aristocratic lady.

Indian Immigration

After the black slaves were freed in 1834, the islands found themselves facing a shortage of farmworkers. In 1845, the wealthy landowners launched a program that brought thousands of immigrants from India as indentured laborers.

These immigrants signed contracts stating that they would work for five years, after which they would be given a bit of land or the money to return home to India. Many of them came hoping to find a better life in Trinidad and Tobago.

But indentured workers were treated almost as poorly as slaves. They lived in crowded, dirty barracks and received little or no medical care.

It wasn't until 1917 that India abolished the indentured labor system. By then many Indians opted to remain in the country, mostly in Trinidad.

Today, East Indians—as they are known to distinguish them from Amerindians—make up about 40 percent of the population. They represent the country's largest ethnic group. Hindu temples are spread across the country, and the traditional holidays of Divali and Phagwa are national celebrations, enjoyed by people of all racial backgrounds.

In 1990 the voters of Trinidad and Tobago made Basdeo Panday the first person of East Indian descent to be elected prime minister.

Trinidad and Tobago's diversity has been its strength, but it has also been the source of conflict. Relations between East Indians and blacks have long been strained. The two communities, for example, have generally supported opposing political parties, and a recent controversy over elections has increased the tension.

Religion

The main faiths of Trinidad and Tobago are Christianity, Hinduism, and Islam. The islands observe the major holidays of each: Easter and Christmas,

A calypso singer holds his instrument. The musical form known as calypso was created on Trindad.

Divali and Phagwa, and Ramadan and Eid ul-Fitr.

In addition, some islanders are followers of Orisha and Spiritual Baptist—religious faiths that incorporate African gods and religious rites with Christian traditions. These religions came from African slaves who maintained their religious traditions even while they were forced to convert to Christianity. Followers believe that good and evil spirits are actively involved in the everyday world. They seek the blessings of spirits through elaborate prayers and offerings.

Education

Trinidad and Tobago's children are required to attend school until they reach the age of 12, and about 70 percent of students continue their education past that age. The country's solid education program has produced a literacy rate approaching 99 percent —among the highest in the region.

The University of the West Indies offers a range of degrees to more than 5,000 students on its Trinidad campus. The university also has campuses in Barbados and Jamaica and serves a dozen Caribbean nations and territories, including Antigua and Barbuda, Grenada, the Cayman Islands, the British Virgin Islands, St. Vincent and the Grenadines, and the Bahamas.

Calypso's Beat

Trinidad and Tobago dances to the rhythms of *calypso* and the steel pan. Trinidad is the birthplace of calypso, a musical style passed down from African slaves centuries ago. Calypso singers tell funny stories about love and life and often include political or satirical messages in their songs.

Aldwyn Roberts (1922–2000), better known as Lord Kitchener, gained fame as the country's greatest calypso singer, with hits such as "Green Fig Man" and "The Beat of the Steelband." When he died after a career spanning more than 60 years, the entire nation mourned.

A modern version of calypso is called *soca*. It is popular in nightclubs and discos.

In the 1940s some resourceful Trinidadians turned over an empty oil drum and transformed it into a musical instrument—the steel pan. These drums, used to play happy, intricate rhythms, can be heard everywhere during Carnival.

A Literary Legacy

For a small country, Trinidad and Tobago has produced its share of brilliant writers. The Nobel Prize–winning poet Derek Walcott (1930–　) was born on Saint Lucia but lived many years in Trinidad. Samuel Selvon (1923–1994) wrote *The Lonely Londoners*, about West Indian immigrants living in England.

One of the world's greatest modern novelists grew up in humble circumstances in the small Trinidadian town of Chaguanas. The grandchild of Indian immigrants to Trinidad, Sir V. S. Naipaul (1932–　) lives in London, but has written often about the place of his birth, including a history of the country.

Naipaul left Trinidad when he was 18 years old to attend Oxford University in England. His first great success, *A House for Mr. Biswas*, was based on his father's life and offers a richly detailed story of small-town

Trinidad. In the book, Mr. Biswas strives to own his own house, a symbol of independence.

Naipaul has traveled the world, and his more than 20 books, including essays and journalism, cover a wide range of subjects. He received the Nobel Prize in literature, the greatest prize an author can win, in 2001. The Nobel Academy paid respect to Naipaul's roots, saying, "It was not until the moment when he decided to explore what he had abandoned (his home in Trinidad) that his writing took off. His childhood street set the tone for him."

In his speech accepting the prize, Naipaul reminisced vividly about his childhood: "I walked from my grandmother's house—past the two or three main-road stores, the Chinese parlour, the Jubilee Theatre, and the high-smelling little Portuguese factory that made cheap blue soap and cheap yellow soap in long bars that were put out to dry and harden in the mornings—every day I walked past these eternal-

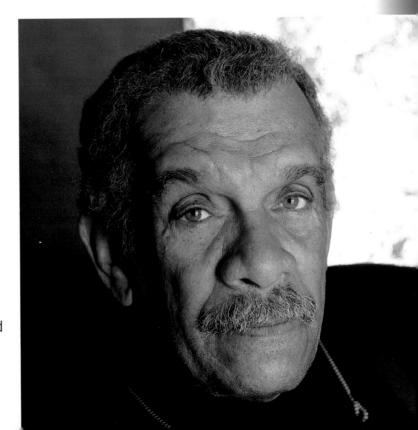

Poet and dramatist Derek Walcott, who won the Nobel Prize in literature in 1992, lived for many years on Trinidad.

seeming things—to the Chaguanas Government School."

No matter that he has lived abroad for 50 years, Naipaul remains a Trinidadian at heart.

Crazy About Cricket

Trinibagonians are zealous fans of their national sport, cricket. For those who have never played or watched it, cricket can be confusing. It bears a similarity to baseball in that it is played with a ball and bat. The game involves two teams that take turns batting and bowling. The bowler throws a ball to knock down a pole called a wicket. The batsman protects the wicket by hitting the ball. The game's rules and strategies can become quite intricate.

Fans across the country keep track of the performances of their favorite

Brian Lara is considered one of the greatest cricket players of all time. A native of Trinidad, he plays for the powerhouse West Indies cricket team.

teams and players in international matches that can last several days. They also love to play, and cricket pitches (playing fields) are found in most large public parks.

Players from the West Indies compete with the best teams from around the world. One of the finest players in the sport's history is a Trinidadian named Brian Lara (1969–   ). He even has a video game named after him!

(Opposite) Port of Spain, Trinidad, is the country's capital and second-largest city. (Right) Poor residents of the islands are likely to live in shantytowns such as the one shown here.

5 The Communities of Trinidad and Tobago

WITH A TOTAL POPULATION slightly less than that of Dallas, Texas, the nation of Trinidad and Tobago has no cities that even approach 100,000 residents. That is not to say, however, that Trinidad and Tobago has no modern, cosmopolitan cities.

Port of Spain

Port of Spain is Trinidad and Tobago's capital. Located in Trinidad's northwest, the city is home to about 49,000 people. The city serves as the business core of the island's major metropolitan area, home to 260,000 inhabitants.

The Arawak Indians who lived in the region in the 1500s called it

Conquerabia because they were able to fight off European settlers.

The present-day city was founded by the Spanish in 1757 when the island's governor moved the colonial capital from St. Joseph. The British seized control of the island in 1797 but kept the city's name.

The city's port and financial district may be the most important areas, but its heart is Woodford Square. Located across from the Red House, where the nation's parliament meets, the square for decades has been a hot spot for political debates and demonstrations. In the 1950s, leaders of the country's independence movement used the square for fiery speeches and rallies.

Port of Spain is a modern, cosmopolitan city with office towers and shopping malls alongside buildings that date back to the colonial era. It also serves as the island's busiest port, a destination for cargo and cruise ships alike.

San Fernando

San Fernando, in the heart of the southern oil country, is Trinidad and Tobago's largest city, with almost 60,000 residents. It is relatively isolated, however, and doesn't compare with Port of Spain as a metropolitan center.

Known as Anaprima by the native tribes, the city lies in the shadow of San Fernando Hill. British explorer Sir Walter Raleigh stopped in the area in 1595 but moved on to search for gold and didn't establish a settlement. The Spanish founded the present-day city in 1784.

San Fernando serves as the major business center for Trinidad's large oil industry. In recent years, city leaders have launched a modernization campaign to spark economic development and attract more jobs to the area.

Scarborough

Scarborough is Tobago's capital and largest city, although it is much smaller than Port of Spain and is less of a financial center.. The town was founded in 1654 by Dutch settlers who dubbed it Lampinsburgh. When the British seized control in 1762, they renamed the town Scarborough. The cannons of Fort King George, built by the British in the 1770s and mostly in ruins today, still overlook Rockly Bay.

A couple of decades after the British, the French took over and changed the name again—to Port Louis. The British later switched the name back.

In some ways an overgrown fishing village, Scarborough is far more laid back than the larger cities and towns of Trinidad. But residents like it that way.

Arima and Chaguanas

Arima and Chaguanas are small towns in Trinidad's interior, but they hold symbolic importance for the island's Carib and East

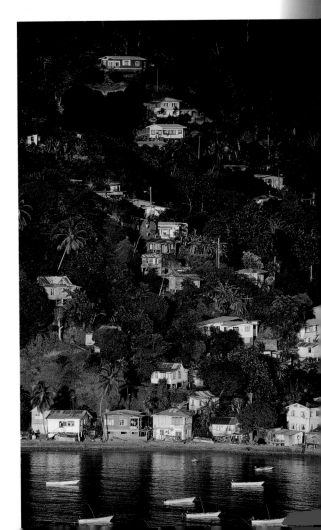

A view of Charlottesville, a small fishing village on Tobago.

Indian communities.

Arima, located east of Port of Spain, got its name from the Arawak word for water. Today it is the home of the island's Santa Rosa Festival, which honors the patron saint of the Carib Indians. The August festival has helped to keep alive the once-fading cultural traditions of the island's indigenous peoples.

The rocky northwest coast of Tobago.

Chaguanas, located near the west coast, got its name from the Chaguanes tribe that lived in the area. The town boomed with the arrival of East Indian farmworkers in the mid-1800s. Today, the Divali Nigar site serves as a center for East Indian culture and holds popular festivals for Divali and Arrival Day.

A Calendar of Trinibagonian Festivals

The holidays of Trinidad and Tobago reflect the many diverse cultures that make up the country's population. There are Christian celebrations, often with an African twist, as well as Hindu and Muslim holidays.

No holiday is bigger than Carnival. Trinibagonians claim they put on the biggest and best Carnival in the Caribbean, and they may just be right. Thousands of tourists travel to Port of Spain every year to join in the good times.

JANUARY

Eid ul-Fitr marks the end of Ramadan, the holiest period in the Muslim calendar. A festive meal on this day signals the end of the sunrise-to-sunset fasting that Muslims have observed during Ramadan. Because Muslims follow a lunar calendar, the actual date of Ramadan changes every year.

FEBRUARY

Carnival in Port of Spain ushers in the Christian season of Lent. Because Lent is a solemn time, Carnival is a last chance for people to let loose.

The wild celebration includes calypso bands and wandering minstrels. Horned devils in blue greasepaint and other traditional Carnival characters in costume mingle with the crowds during the all-night partying.

Trinidadians take their Carnival extremely seriously and begin the preparations and the partying right after the New Year, giving them time to build up to a frenzied climax on the two days before Ash Wednesday, which marks the beginning of Lent. In certain years Carnival takes place during March.

MARCH

Hindus mark spring by celebrating **Phagwa**, but people of all religious backgrounds join the dancing and singing of traditional folk songs called *chowtals*. As part of the festivities, participants playfully soak each other with purple-colored water called *abeer*—a symbolic reminder of spring's arrival.

APRIL

Hosay takes place between March and June, depending on the year. This Muslim holiday marks the deaths of the prophet Muhammad's grandsons. Originally a solemn holiday, Hosay has evolved into a festive occasion. Drumming and dancing fill the streets during the four-day festival, whose climax comes when marchers ceremonially toss bamboo coffins called *tadjahs* into the sea.

MAY

The Buccoo Goat and Crab Races after Easter are among the most unusual and popular events on Tobago. Race fans place bets on their favorite goats and urge the specially trained animals to the finish line. The crab races are more chaotic, given the difficulty of keeping the creatures on track, but just as much fun.

May 30, **Arrival Day,** commemorates the

A Calendar of Trinibagonian Festivals

beginning of the mass migration of Indian laborers to Trinidad in the 1840s.

JUNE

The Fisherman's Festival in Tobago honors the feast day of St. Peter on June 29. The entire island marks the occasion with festivities honoring the local fishermen, but the largest celebration is in Charlottesville.

JULY

Tobago Heritage Festival celebrates the island's history and culture. A highlight is the "Ole Time Wedding"—a mock wedding incorporating British and African traditions, during which groom and bride parade through the streets.

AUGUST

August 1, **Emancipation Day,** marks the end of slavery throughout the British-controlled Caribbean in 1834. African traditions are honored on this day.

The Santa Rosa Festival, which begins August 1, celebrates Trinidad's Amerindian heritage with native foods and a procession honoring St. Rose that winds through the streets of Arima. A highlight is the crowning of the festival's Carib queen.

OCTOBER

Divali, the Hindu Festival of Light, begins in late October and extends into November. During this time, Hindus celebrating good's triumph over evil light candles as offerings to Mother Lakshmi, the goddess of light.

NOVEMBER

The Pan Jazz Festival in Port of Spain is a major event for lovers of steel pan music. The island's finest pan players jam with jazz musicians to entertain the crowds.

DECEMBER

The music of *parang* marks the **Christmas** holiday season. In a legacy of Spain's long rule, roving bands of minstrels treat their neighbors to traditional holiday tunes.

The country also marks **Boxing Day**, the day after Christmas. For this traditionally British holiday that falls on December 26, many families exchange gifts.

51

Recipes

Trinidad *Pelau*

2 cups rice
2 lbs chicken or beef, cut into bite-size pieces
2 tbsp vegetable oil
1 tbsp soy sauce
salt and pepper to taste
4 1/2 cups water
1 tbsp sugar
1/2 cup minced onions
1 clove garlic, chopped
1/2 cup chopped celery stalks
1/2 cup chopped tomatoes
1 green chili pepper
mango chutney

Directions:
1. Season chicken with salt and pepper.
2. Heat oil in saucepan. Add sugar and heat until blackened.
3. Add seasoned chicken. Stir, cover, and cook for 10 minutes over low heat.
4. Add onions, celery, finely chopped garlic, tomatoes, and rice. Stir.
5. Add water, soy sauce, and whole pepper. Bring to a boil.
6. Cover and simmer for 40 minutes.
 Serve with chutney.

Curried Chicken Wings

24 chicken wings
1 cup coconut milk
2 cups instant mashed potato mix
2 tbsp curry powder
6 tbsp melted margarine
2 minced garlic cloves

Directions:
1. Rinse chicken wings and pat dry. Cut chicken wings apart at both joints.
2. In large bowl, add wings to coconut milk, and stir well. Cover and refrigerate for 2–3 hours.
3. In another bowl, combine potato mix and curry powder.
4. Drain wings and roll in potato mixture, one at a time, to coat.
5. Arrange wings in greased baking pans.
6. Combine melted margarine and garlic and pour over chicken.
7. Bake uncovered in oven at 375 degrees for 45 minutes or until well browned.

Recipes

Chicken *Tandoori*
1 whole chicken (3–4 pounds)
2 tbsp lemon juice
1/2 tsp salt
1 cup yogurt
2 tsp paprika powder
2 tsp coriander powder
2 tsp cumin powder
1 tsp ginger powder
4 crushed garlic cloves
3 tsp vegetable oil
1 tsp salt
juice of one lemon
red food coloring

Directions:
1. Wash and skin chicken; discard giblets.
2. Prick chicken all over with sharp kitchen knife.
3. Combine lemon juice and salt and rub mixture into chicken. Marinate 30 minutes.
4. Mix paprika, cumin, coriander, ginger, salt, garlic, yogurt, and oil. Rub chicken thoroughly inside and outside with the mixture and marinate 6–8 hours.
5. Place in oven preheated to 450 degrees. Roast for 50 minutes.
6. Combine lemon juice and a few drops of the red food coloring. Remove chicken and rub on mixture. Return to oven and cook 10 more minutes.

Phoulorie
2 cups split pea powder
1/2 cup flour
1 garlic clove, crushed
1 1/2 tsp salt
black pepper
2 tsp curry powder
2 tsp baking powder
vegetable oil for deep frying

Directions:
1. Mix split pea powder with all ingredients except water.
2. Add just enough water to make a thick, smooth batter.
3. Heat oil in heavy pot over high heat. Drop batter, a teaspoon at a time, into the oil and let cook until brown.
4. Drain and test one for salt and dryness. If too dry, add a little water to the batter.
5. Serve with chutney.

Glossary

Amerindians—Native Americans.

asphalt—a tarlike substance, found in natural deposits or obtained as a by-product of petroleum refining, that is used as a paving material.

caciques—Native chieftains, especially in regions explored or conquered by the Spanish.

calypso—a type of music popular throughout the Caribbean that originated in Trinidad and that often pokes fun at local political figures and events.

cassava—a plant whose starchy root is used to make bread.

conquistadors—Spanish military leaders who explored and conquered the territories of Latin America beginning in the 16th century.

coup—the sudden seizure of a government by a small group, using violence or the threat of violence.

gross domestic product (GDP)—the total value of goods and services produced by a country in a one-year period.

indentured—bound by contract to work for a certain employer for a specified period of time, often for very low wages and under restrictive conditions.

indigenous—native or original to a particular region.

inflation—increases in consumer prices over a period of time.

islets—small islands.

metropolitan area—a region composed of a city and its surrounding suburbs.

parang—a type of music, originally from Spain, that is played especially by roving bands of musicians during the Christmas season.

patois—a distinct manner of speaking that is characterized by special vocabulary and that often incorporates words from several different languages.

privatize—to place government-owned commercial enterprises into the hands of private investors.

reserve—an area of land set aside for the preservation of native plants and wildlife.

soca—a West Indian musical form related to calypso that is especially popular in nightclubs.

trade winds—prevailing winds of the Tropics that blow toward the equator.

Project and Report Ideas

Movie Review

Do some library research about the real legend of El Dorado, the fabled city of gold. Rent and watch the movie *The Road to Eldorado*. Write a two-page report in which you compare history with the film. What elements did the movie's makers draw from history and what did they completely make up?

Carnival Map

Carnival celebrations are popular around much of the world. Some major celebrations take place in Rio de Janeiro in Brazil, New Orleans in Louisiana, and Port of Spain in Trinidad. Draw a map of the Americas with those three cities highlighted. In the margins, describe five distinctive customs of each of the celebrations. Make sure to include differences and similarities.

British Empire Map

The British Empire once stretched across much of the world. At one time, each of the following countries was a colony of Great Britain: the United States, Canada, Jamaica, Trinidad and Tobago, Nigeria, Zimbabwe, India, Pakistan, Australia, New Zealand. Draw a world map, locating each of these countries, naming their most important independence movement leaders, and listing the years they finally gained independence.

Crafts

- Using construction paper and other art materials, create your own Carnival mask. Write a short description of the character or creature you mean to represent.
- Design and write a foldout travel brochure for Trinidad and Tobago. Highlight three or four reasons tourists should visit the islands (don't forget to include Tobago). Use your own drawings to illustrate.

Project and Report Ideas

Holiday Reports

Select a popular Trinibagonian holiday to learn more about and write a one-page report about its origins and customs. Consider one of the following holidays: Hosay, Eid ul-Fitr, Divali, Phagwa.

Immigrant Stories

The people of Trinidad and Tobago come from all over the world—Europe, Africa, and India. Present an oral report telling the story of how you or your ancestors came to live in the United States. If you don't know the details of your own family's story, talk generally about the immigration of people from a foreign country in your family's background.

Cricket Match

Learn about the rules of cricket. Draw up instructions on how to play a simplified version of the game. Help to organize the class into teams and play a match. You can improvise with the equipment, using baseball bats or balls.

Chronology

Ca. 1000 B.C.	First inhabitants of islands arrive from South America.
Ca. 300 B.C.	Arawak Indians establish themselves on Trinidad.
A.D. 1400	The rival Arawak and Carib Indians share the islands.
1498	Christopher Columbus lands on Trinidad, which he names for three hills, but bypasses Tobago.
1592	Spain establishes its first settlement in Trinidad.
1654	A group of Latvians establish the first European settlement on Tobago.
1797	British seize control of Trinidad.
1802	France and Spain give up any claims to Trinidad and Tobago, which officially become separate colonies of Great Britain.
1834	British abolish slavery.
1845	First wave of indentured workers arrives in Trinidad from India.
1899	Trinidad and Tobago are joined as a single government.
1916	Practice of indenturing workers abolished by India.
1962	Trinidad and Tobago becomes an independent commonwealth with Eric Williams as prime minister.
1963	Hurricane Flora devastates Tobago, killing 20 and destroying plantations.
1970s	International oil crisis leads to unprecedented economic expansion in Trinidad and Tobago.
1976	Country becomes a republic.
1990	Muslim radicals revolt against government but are forced to surrender.

1995	Basdeo Panday becomes country's first prime minister of East Indian descent.
2001	Trinidadian novelist V. S. Naipaul wins the Nobel Prize in literature; national elections end in a deadlock, and Patrick Manning is eventually named prime minister over Panday.
2002	The government announced plans to spend more than $200 million on construction and development projects on Tobago in the upcoming years.
2003	Trinidad and Tobago's state-owned sugar company closes down, leaving over 8,000 without jobs.
2004	Trinidad and Tobago signs an agreement with Venezuela to develop South America's largest natural-gas field, the offshore Deltana Platform field, which is located under the waters of both countries.
2005	At least 10,000 people march in front of the Parliament building in Port of Spain, calling government attention to Trinidad and Tobago's high rates of violent crime.
2006	Basdeo Panday is sentenced to prison time for violating banking laws; the conviction is later overturned.
2007	Patrick Manning's party, the People's National Movement, is re-elected.
2008	Manning opponents in Parliament raise a vote of no confidence against him; he survives the vote and remains in office.
2010	In May, Kamla Persad-Bissessar is sworn in as the country's first female prime minister.

Further Reading/Internet Resources

Besson, Gerard. *Folklore & Legends of Trinidad and Tobago.* Cascade, Trinidad: Paria Publishing, 2007.

Ganeshram, Ramin. *Sweet Hands: Island Cooking from Trinidad and Tobago.* New York: Hippocrene Books, 2006.

Green, Garth L., and Philip W. Scher. *Trinidad Carnival: The Cultural Politics of a Transnational Festival.* Bloomington.: Indiana University Press, 2007.

Robinson, A. N. R. *The Mechanics of Independence: Patterns of Political and Economic Transformation in Trinidad and Tobago.* Kingston, Jamaica: University of the West Indies Press, 2001.

Smailes, Alex, and Jeremy Taylor. *Trinidad & Tobago: Carnival, Land, Water, People.* Oxford, UK: Macmillan Education, 2006.

Travel Information

http://www.meppublishers.com/online/discover/trinidad/index.php
http://www.gotrinidadandtobago.com/home/home.php

History and Geography

http://www.centrelink.org/Trinidad_Tobago.html

Economic and Political Information

http://www.travel.state.gov/travel/trinidad_tobago.html
http://www.gov.tt

Culture and Festivals

http://www.pantrinbago.com
http://www.tobagowi.com/culture/cultlink.htm

Publisher's Note: The websites listed on this page were active at the time of publication. The publisher is not responsible for websites that have changed their address or discontinued operation since the date of publication. The publisher reviews and updates the websites each time the book is reprinted.

For More Information

Tourism and Industrial Development Company (Trinidad and Tobago)
P.O. Box 222
10-14 Philipps St.
Port of Spain
Trinidad, West Indies
(868) 623-6022/3

Trinidad and Tobago Embassy
1708 Massachusetts Ave., NW
Washington, DC 20036-1975
(202) 467-6490

United States Embassy to Trinidad and Tobago
15 Queen's Park West
Port of Spain
Trinidad & Tobago
(868) 622-6371/6

Index

Index/Picture Credits

Contributors

Senior Consulting Editor **James D. Henderson** is professor of international studies at Coastal Carolina University. He is the author of *Conservative Thought in Twentieth Century Latin America: The Ideals of Laureano Gómez* (1988; Spanish edition *Las ideas de Laureano Gómez* published in 1985); *When Colombia Bled: A History of the Violence in Tolima* (1985; Spanish edition *Cuando Colombia se desangró, una historia de la Violencia en metrópoli y provincia*, 1984); and coauthor of *A Reference Guide to Latin American History* (2000) and *Ten Notable Women of Latin America* (1978).

Mr. Henderson earned a bachelor's degree in history from Centenary College of Louisiana, and a master's degree in history from the University of Arizona. He then spent three years in the Peace Corps, serving in Colombia, before earning his doctorate in Latin American history in 1972 at Texas Christian University.

Romel Hernandez is a freelance writer and editor based in Oregon. He was born in New Jersey and graduated from Yale. He is an award-winning daily newspaper journalist who has worked in New Jersey, Colorado, and Oregon.